LEARN TO PLAY
DRUMS

Eileen O'Brien

Designed by Neil Francis

Studio photography by Howard Allman
Original music by Clive Fenner
Additional music by Nigel Hooper

Edited by Caroline Hooper

Drums consultants: Clive Fenner and Neil Findlay
Music setting: David Kear
Series editor: Jane Chisholm

THE DRUM SET

This book will help you to get the most out of your drum set, whether you are a complete beginner or you already know how to play.

It contains music in lots of different styles, and there are hints about everything from practicing to looking after your drums. You can find out about famous drummers, and there is helpful advice on making up your own music and playing in a band.

Drum sets

Drum sets are made up of a number of drums and cymbals. There are usually three different types of drums: a snare drum, a bass drum and tom toms (often called 'toms'). Each drum makes a different sound.

There are also three main categories of cymbals, known as ride, crash and hi-hat. The number of drums and cymbals in a set varies from player to player, but here you can see the items used in a fairly typical set.

Crash cymbal

Ride cymbal

Small rack tom (or high tom)

Medium rack tom (or mid tom)

Hi-hat cymbals

Snare drum

Bass drum

Don't worry if your set doesn't have all of these drums and cymbals. You can still play all the music in this book.

How the sound is produced

Drums are made by stretching a piece of material, usually plastic, over a round frame. This plastic surface is called the drumhead. When you strike a drumhead or a cymbal, it vibrates, causing the air around it to move. These air vibrations are called sound waves. When you strike a drum, some of the sound waves spread down into the hollow part of the drum, where they echo around and grow louder. This is known as resonating.

A drum set with five drums, like this one, is called a five-piece set.

Floor tom (or low tom)

Drum stool

Born in England in 1951, **Phil Collins** first made his mark as the drummer in the band Genesis. As a left-handed player, his drums are set up the other way around to most sets. You can find out more about playing left-handed on page 10.

Choosing a drum set

It is often cheaper to buy a whole drum set, rather than buying each item separately. If you know an experienced drummer, it's a good idea to take him or her along with you. Here are some things to look for when buying a second-hand set:

Checklist for choosing a drum set

- Check that the drums and stands are not damaged in any way, and the metal fittings are not rusty or painted over.

- Make sure you can adjust and tighten all the stands easily and securely. Check that the foot pedals are working correctly.

- The frame of each drum should be perfectly round with no dents or cracks. Check the cymbals for cracks too.

- Check the snare drum in particular. When you strike it, it should make a tight, clear sound with no rattling noises.

Drums

Some drums have just one drumhead. This type of drum is known as a single-headed drum. Drums that have a head at both ends of the frame are known as double-headed drums. The round frame of a drum is usually wooden or metal, and is called the drumshell.

Some drums sound higher or lower than others. How high or low a drum sounds is called its pitch. The larger and deeper a drum is, the lower its pitch.

The drumhead is held in place by a round hoop, called a counterhoop, or rim.

Drumhead

Drumshell

The drumhead that you strike to make a sound (the top drumhead) is called the batter head.

The edge of the drumshell at each end is called the bearing edge. The drumhead and rim rest on top of the bearing edge.

In double-headed drums, the drumhead opposite the batter head is called the resonator head. This head is not meant to be struck, and is slightly different from the batter head (see page 30). In the case of the snare drum, the resonator head is called the snare head, after the layer of wires, called snares, that lie across it.

Tension screws used to tighten the drumhead.

Tension brackets are used to keep the counterhoop in place and stretch each drumhead across the shell.

Born in the USA in 1962, **Chad Smith** joined the Red Hot Chilli Peppers in 1989. The band's music is a mixture of heavy metal and rap, and Smith's aggressive playing style is well-suited to their energetic live shows.

Drums in a drum set

The stands and holders that keep the drums and cymbals in place are known as the hardware. This term also refers to the foot pedals that are used to play some of the drums and cymbals.

There are lots of different types of hardware available, but most stands and holders work in a similar way. Here you can see the drums and their stands used in a set: the snare drum, bass drum and toms of different sizes. Each tom makes the same type of sound, but different sizes produce different pitches. Below you can learn about three toms: the floor tom and two smaller toms called rack toms. The rack toms are usually positioned on top of the bass drum.

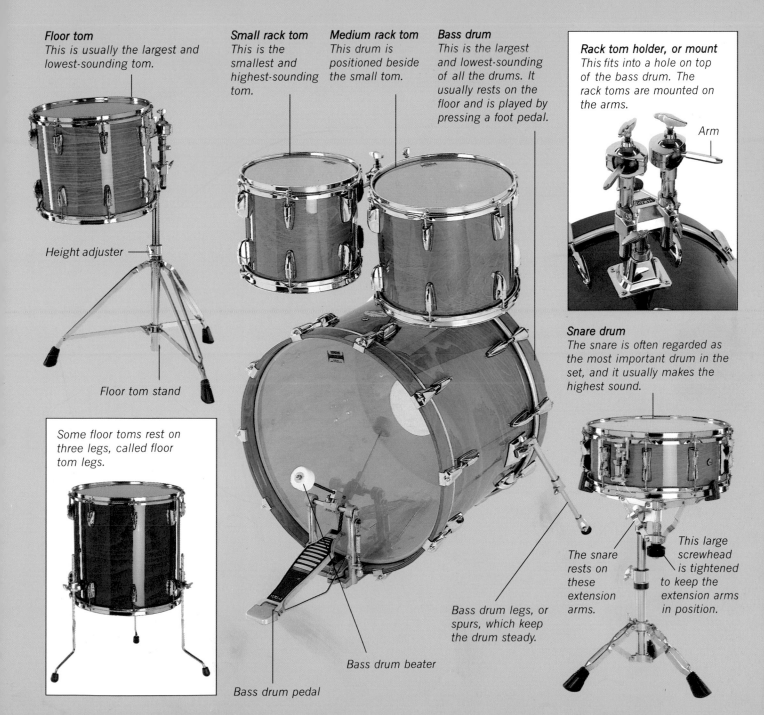

Floor tom
This is usually the largest and lowest-sounding tom.

Small rack tom
This is the smallest and highest-sounding tom.

Medium rack tom
This drum is positioned beside the small tom.

Bass drum
This is the largest and lowest-sounding of all the drums. It usually rests on the floor and is played by pressing a foot pedal.

Rack tom holder, or mount
This fits into a hole on top of the bass drum. The rack toms are mounted on the arms.

Arm

Height adjuster

Floor tom stand

Some floor toms rest on three legs, called floor tom legs.

Snare drum
The snare is often regarded as the most important drum in the set, and it usually makes the highest sound.

The snare rests on these extension arms.

This large screwhead is tightened to keep the extension arms in position.

Bass drum legs, or spurs, which keep the drum steady.

Bass drum beater

Bass drum pedal

Cymbals

Cymbals used in a drum set come in different weights and sizes. The sound is made when the cymbal is struck. You can make different sounds by striking a cymbal in different places, and by using cymbals of different sizes. As a general rule, the larger the cymbal, the louder it will sound. Here you can see the main parts of a cymbal.

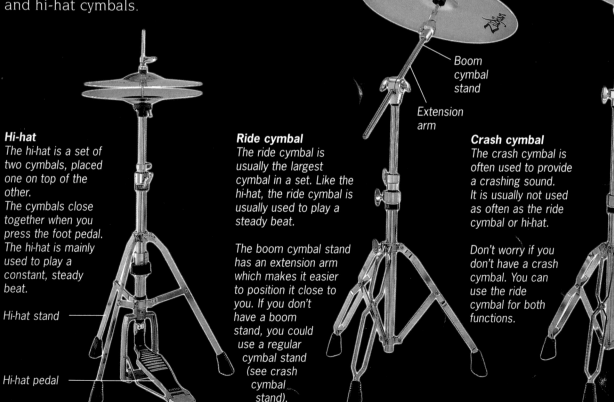

A hole to mount the cymbal on a stand

The raised part in the middle is called the cup, or bell. You can make different sounds by using cymbals with different sized bells.

The area from the bell to the edge of the cymbal is called the bow, or taper.

Cymbals in a drum set

Here you can learn about the main cymbals and their stands in a basic drum set: the ride, crash and hi-hat cymbals.

Boom cymbal stand

Extension arm

Angle adjuster

Regular cymbal stand

Hi-hat
The hi-hat is a set of two cymbals, placed one on top of the other.
The cymbals close together when you press the foot pedal. The hi-hat is mainly used to play a constant, steady beat.

Hi-hat stand

Hi-hat pedal

Ride cymbal
The ride cymbal is usually the largest cymbal in a set. Like the hi-hat, the ride cymbal is usually used to play a steady beat.

The boom cymbal stand has an extension arm which makes it easier to position it close to you. If you don't have a boom stand, you could use a regular cymbal stand (see crash cymbal stand).

Crash cymbal
The crash cymbal is often used to provide a crashing sound. It is usually not used as often as the ride cymbal or hi-hat.

Don't worry if you don't have a crash cymbal. You can use the ride cymbal for both functions.

Cymbal stands

It is important that the cymbal doesn't touch the metal of the stand as this can cause it to crack. To prevent this, some parts of the stands are covered with plastic and felt. Below you can find out how to fix these attachments to the stands.

These are the pieces of plastic and felt you will need for your cymbal stands.

Ride and crash plastic sleeve

Ride and crash felt washer

Hi-hat felt washer

Fitting the crash and ride cymbals

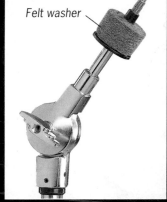
Threads
Felt washer
Plastic sleeve

1. Fit a plastic sleeve over the threads at the top of the stand.

2. Place a felt washer over the sleeve, as shown in the picture.

Wingnut
Felt washer

3. Place the cymbal on the stand so it rests on the washer.

4. Put another washer on top, before gently tightening the wingnut.

Fitting the hi-hat

The lower hi-hat cymbal is usually heavier than the upper one. Sometimes the upper and lower cymbals are labelled, so it's easy to tell which one is which. The lower cymbal rests on a plastic holder, as well as a rubber and a felt washer.

This is called a clutch. It holds the upper cymbal in place.
Felt washers
Clutch nut
Wingnut

1. The upper cymbal fits in between the two felt washers on the clutch. Tighten the clutch nut to keep the upper cymbal in place, then slide the clutch over the shaft on top of the lower cymbal.

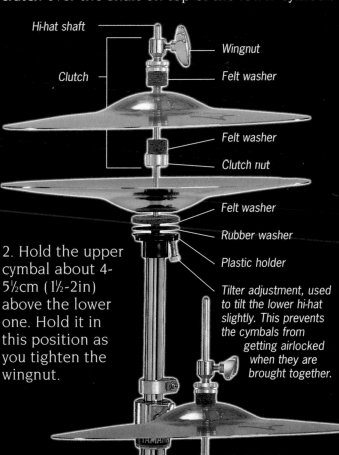
Hi-hat shaft
Clutch
Wingnut
Felt washer
Felt washer
Clutch nut
Felt washer
Rubber washer
Plastic holder
Tilter adjustment, used to tilt the lower hi-hat slightly. This prevents the cymbals from getting airlocked when they are brought together.

2. Hold the upper cymbal about 4-5½cm (1½-2in) above the lower one. Hold it in this position as you tighten the wingnut.

DRUMSTICKS

Drumsticks come in different shapes and sizes, and the type you use affects the sound you produce from your drum set. You can learn about some different types on this page.

Types of drumstick

Most sticks are made from wood. The top of a stick is known as the bead, or tip. This is the part that is usually used to strike a drum or cymbal. The tip can be wooden or nylon. Sticks with wooden tips make a slightly different sound from those with nylon tips. Try out each type before you decide which one to use.

Wooden tip drumstick	Nylon tip drumstick

Here you can see the main parts of a drumstick.

Checklist for choosing drumsticks

- Test that drumsticks are straight by rolling them along a flat surface. If they roll smoothly, the sticks are straight, but if the tips wobble, the sticks are warped and are no good.

- Your drumsticks should not be too heavy or too light. Most drumsticks have sizes marked on them in the form of a number followed by a letter. A good size to start with is '5B'.

- Make sure that both sticks have the same brand name and size marked on them.

Tip   Neck   Shoulder   Shaft   Butt

Sitting at your drum set

As you play your drum set, you should be able to reach all the drums and cymbals easily without stretching too far. Assemble your drums around your body rather than the other way around.

You can find out how to set your equipment up on pages 10-11. First, though, you need to make sure you are sitting correctly on your drum stool. Most drum stools have height adjusters, so you can adjust the height to suit yourself. If you don't have an actual drum stool, use a chair or stool of the right height for you.

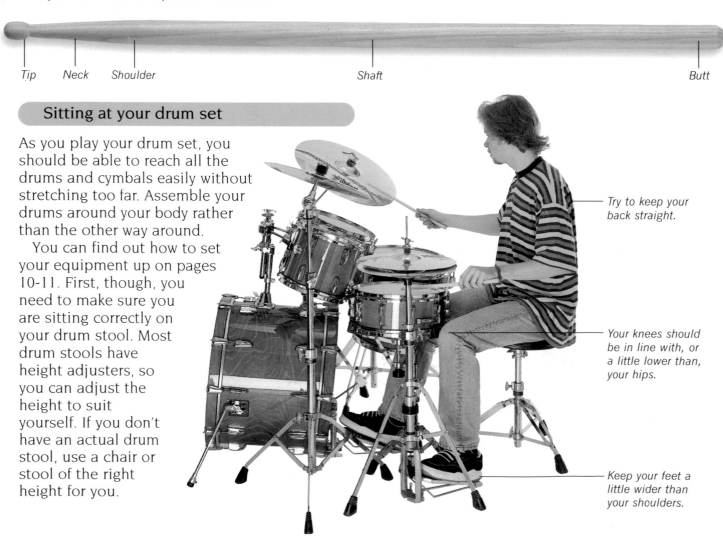

Try to keep your back straight.

Your knees should be in line with, or a little lower than, your hips.

Keep your feet a little wider than your shoulders.

Holding your drumsticks

The way you hold your drumsticks affects the way you assemble your set. You need to be able to reach all the drums and cymbals while holding your sticks comfortably. Most drummers use one of two ways to hold, or grip, their sticks. These are called the matched grip and the traditional grip. You can use either of these grips, depending on what feels most natural.

The matched grip

This grip is called the matched grip because both drumsticks are held in the same way.

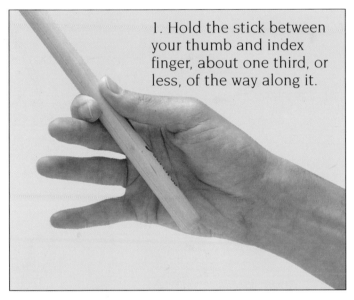

1. Hold the stick between your thumb and index finger, about one third, or less, of the way along it.

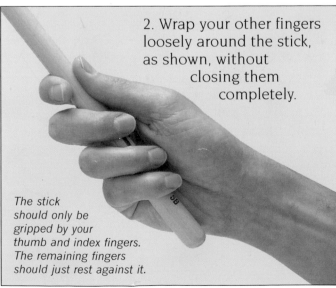

2. Wrap your other fingers loosely around the stick, as shown, without closing them completely.

The stick should only be gripped by your thumb and index fingers. The remaining fingers should just rest against it.

The traditional grip

For this grip, hold your right stick as for the matched grip, and your left stick as follows:

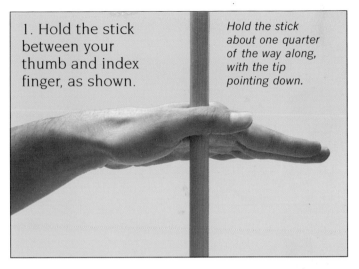

1. Hold the stick between your thumb and index finger, as shown.

Hold the stick about one quarter of the way along, with the tip pointing down.

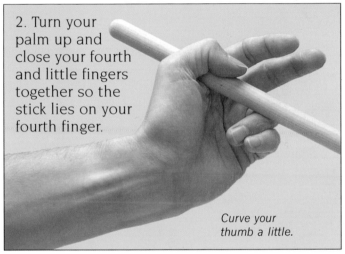

2. Turn your palm up and close your fourth and little fingers together so the stick lies on your fourth finger.

Curve your thumb a little.

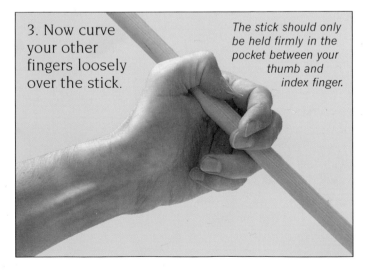

3. Now curve your other fingers loosely over the stick.

The stick should only be held firmly in the pocket between your thumb and index finger.

The way you assemble your drums depends on your size and the way you grip your drumsticks. In general, the items used most often should be closest to you, and those used less often should be farther away. When you position each item, sit on your stool in the correct position, holding your drumsticks, and check that you can reach each item without stretching too far. Here are some guidelines to help you set up.

Positioning your drums

1. Place the bass drum on the floor, with the batter head facing your stool. Extend the spurs evenly on either side, so that the resonator head is raised slightly off the floor.

2. Lift the batter-head side of the bass drum a little and slide the bass drum pedal underneath. Fasten it firmly in place on the counterhoop. Position your stool in front so that, when you sit on it, your right foot is in line with the pedal.

3. As you sit at your set, the small rack tom should be on the left of the bass drum, while the medium rack tom should be on the right.

4. To begin with, you could line up the right edge of the snare drum with the right edge of the small rack tom.

5. Put the floor tom on the right side, at roughly the same height as the snare. Make sure it is close enough to reach with both drumsticks.

Positioning your cymbals

1. Set up the hi-hat as shown on page 7. Place the hi-hat stand on the left-hand side, so that you can press the bass pedal with your right foot, and the hi-hat pedal with your left foot.

2. Put the ride cymbal on the right side, behind the floor tom. Adjust the height so you can play it with your right drumstick.

3. The crash cymbal can be farther away from you, as it is not used as often as other parts of the set. It's usually placed to the left of the small rack tom, behind the hi-hat.

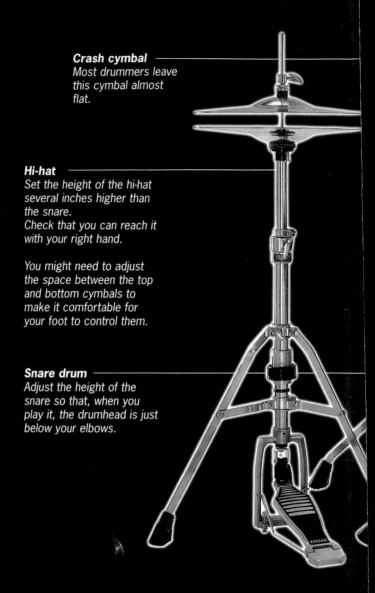

Crash cymbal
Most drummers leave this cymbal almost flat.

Hi-hat
*Set the height of the hi-hat several inches higher than the snare.
Check that you can reach it with your right hand.*

You might need to adjust the space between the top and bottom cymbals to make it comfortable for your foot to control them.

Snare drum
Adjust the height of the snare so that, when you play it, the drumhead is just below your elbows.

Left-handed players

Most of the instructions in this book are for right-handed players. If you are left-handed, you could use the setup shown on these two pages, or you could reverse it (put the hi-hat and the crash cymbal on the right side instead of the left, and so on).

The same goes for the playing instructions. There is no one correct way to play your drum set, so how you play it is up to you. You could begin by setting your drums up as shown in the picture above. If you find it difficult to play, try experimenting with different ways of setting up and playing until you find the best way for you.

Ride cymbal
This cymbal is usually tilted towards the player.

If your set only has one cymbal, set it up as for the ride cymbal.

Rack toms
Adjust the position of the rack toms so you don't have to reach too far.

Tilt the rack toms towards you slightly.

Floor tom
The floor tom is often easier to play if it is tilted towards you. If your floor tom rests on legs, you can tilt it by having the legs at different heights.

Bass drum
Make sure you can reach the bass pedal with your right foot.

Checklist for setting up

- Try to assemble your drums and cymbals on a carpeted surface. This stops the stands from sliding away from you.

- If you move your set from place to place, you could bring your own piece of carpet with you. By marking the position of each item on the carpet with some tape, you can use the same setup each time you play.

- Be careful to not overtighten any of the wingnuts or fittings, especially the wingnuts on your cymbal stands, as this can damage your hardware, as well as your drums and cymbals. It also affects the sound that your cymbals make.

- As you begin to play, you may need to change the positions and angles of your drums and cymbals, until you find the most comfortable position.

STRIKING A DRUM

The way you strike your drum depends on whether you use the matched or traditional grips. The strokes described here can be used for most of the drums and cymbals in your set (also known as surfaces), but you could try practicing on your snare drum first. Strike the drumhead near the center.

The matched grip drum stroke

If you use the matched grip, both hands strike the surface in the same way. It's a good idea to practice with each hand separately for a while, before alternating the right and left strokes.

1. Hold your stick about 5½cm (2in) above the drum. For the right stroke, keep your thumb to the left of the stick. For the left stroke, keep your thumb to the right. Bend your wrist to raise the stick up. As the stick moves up it should be gripped by your thumb and first finger. Your other fingers should be wrapped lightly around it.

2. Now relax your wrist and allow the stick to drop straight down so that it bounces off the drumhead. Use your fingers to control the stick, so it stops about 5½cm (2in) above the drumhead. Try not to grip it too tightly.

The traditional grip drum stroke

If you use the traditional grip, both hands strike the drum in different ways. The right-hand stroke is the same as the matched grip stroke. Here you can find out how to strike a drum with your left hand, using the traditional grip.

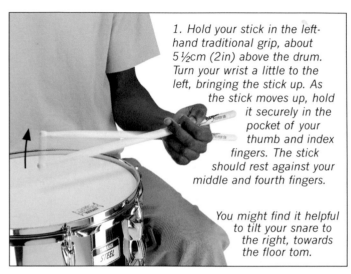

1. Hold your stick in the left-hand traditional grip, about 5½cm (2in) above the drum. Turn your wrist a little to the left, bringing the stick up. As the stick moves up, hold it securely in the pocket of your thumb and index fingers. The stick should rest against your middle and fourth fingers.

You might find it helpful to tilt your snare to the right, towards the floor tom.

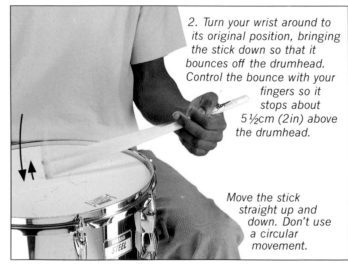

2. Turn your wrist around to its original position, bringing the stick down so that it bounces off the drumhead. Control the bounce with your fingers so it stops about 5½cm (2in) above the drumhead.

Move the stick straight up and down. Don't use a circular movement.

The snare drum

When a snare drum is struck, the wire snares rattle against the snare head. The snares are connected to a lever on the side of the drum, called the snare throw-off switch. By moving this lever, you can pull the snares tight against the head (this is called having the snares on) or loosen them (having the snares off).

Snare throw-off switch

Tension bolt used to tighten the snares.

Playing with the snares off is often associated with Latin music (see page 38).

Snares

READING MUSIC

Musical notes are written on a set of five lines called a staff, or stave. In drum music, there is a special sign at the beginning of the staff, called a clef. There are many different types of clef, but this one is usually used to indicate instruments that you strike. These are known as percussion instruments. Each item in a set has its own line or space on the staff. Drums are shown as notes (see below) and cymbals are shown as crosses. Here you can see where each one is written.

The bass and snare drums are written in the spaces between the staff lines.

The tom toms are written on the lines.

The cymbals are written as crosses.

Drums and cymbals may be shown in different places on the staff in other books.

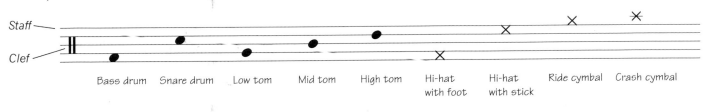

Staff

Clef

Bass drum · Snare drum · Low tom · Mid tom · High tom · Hi-hat with foot · Hi-hat with stick · Ride cymbal · Crash cymbal

How long notes last

The length of a note is measured by counting. Each count is called a beat. The shape of a note tells you how many beats that note lasts for. The pattern of beats in a piece is called its rhythm.

A quarter note, or crotchet, lasts for one beat.

A half note, or minim, lasts for two beats.

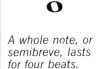

A whole note, or semibreve, lasts for four beats.

Grouping notes together

Music is divided into sections called measures, each containing an equal number of beats. Each measure is separated from the next by a line called a bar line. At the beginning of the staff, a sign called a time signature tells you how many beats there are in each measure, and what kind of beats they are. On the right, you can learn about a time signature called four-four time.

The number 4 at the top tells you there are four beats in each measure.

Bar line

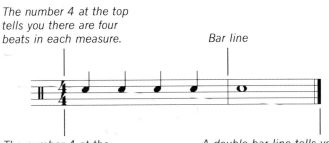

The number 4 at the bottom tells you they are quarter notes.

A double bar line tells you that you have reached the end of the music.

Starting to play

Here is a short rhythm for you to play on your snare drum. The letters over the music tell you which hand to use for each note. These are known as stickings. The 'R' means play with your right hand, and the 'L' means play with your left hand. Make sure that each stroke sounds the same, by lifting each stick the same height above the drumhead.

It will help if you count to four before you begin.

Try to keep counting as you play.

13

PLAYING THE RIDE CYMBAL

The ride cymbal is often used to play a steady, constant rhythm pattern, acting as a timekeeper, while other drums and cymbals play different rhythms around it.

Play the ride cymbal with your right hand, using the right-hand drum stroke described on page 12. Strike it on the bow with the tip of your drumstick, around 6-8cm (2-3in) in from the edge. You might need to change the angle of your ride cymbal to play it comfortably.

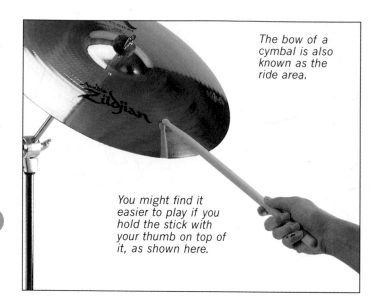

The bow of a cymbal is also known as the ride area.

You might find it easier to play if you hold the stick with your thumb on top of it, as shown here.

Rhythm: Jumpin' in

For this piece, play the snare with your left hand and the ride cymbal with your right hand. Make sure you can reach both surfaces comfortably.

Two or more surfaces to be played together are written one above the other on the staff.

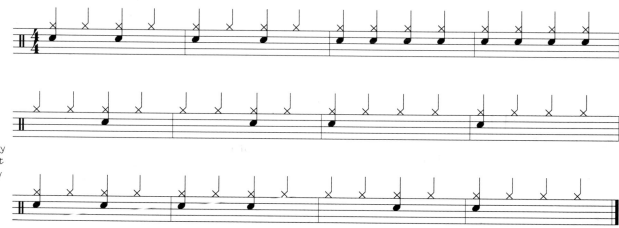

When you can play this piece without any mistakes, try playing it a little faster.

Born in the USA in 1954, **Peter Erskine** began playing drums at the age of four. He had established his reputation as an outstanding jazz-rock drummer and teacher by the early 1970s. During the 70s, he played with several world-class jazz groups, before joining Weather Report in 1978. He has played for many famous artists, including Steely Dan and Joni Mitchell, and has played on over 250 albums.

USING YOUR FEET

Playing the bass drum

There are many different ways to operate the bass pedal. Most drummers, however, use one of the methods described here.

The first method is good for playing quietly and fairly slowly, because you have more control over the pedal. The second method is good for loud, fast playing. Some drummers change the way they operate the bass pedal during a piece.

For the first method (see below), keep your foot flat on the pedal at all times. To press the pedal down, put pressure on your entire foot. You should release the pedal immediately after the beater has struck the drum, so that the beater is around 5cm (2in) away from the drumhead.

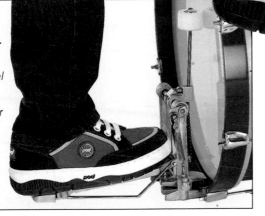

Press the pedal with your right foot.

Keep your heel at the bottom of the pedal and move your foot from your ankle.

For the second method (see above), place the ball of your foot around halfway down the pedal, keeping your heel up. To play, lift your whole foot off the pedal, then bounce your leg on the ball of your foot.

Sounds and silences

As well as sounds, music also contains silences. There are symbols called rests that tell you how long these silences last. When you see one in a piece, count the correct number of beats before you play the next note.

𝄽   *A quarter rest lasts for one quarter beat.*

▬   *A half rest lasts for two quarter beats.*

▬   *A whole rest lasts for four quarter beats.*

Rhythm: Bottom heavy

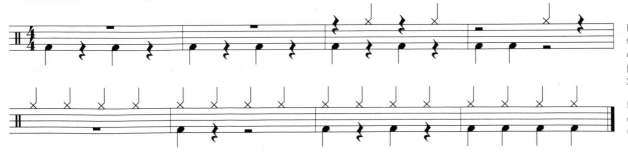

Here you might find it easier to operate the bass pedal by keeping your foot flat.

Play the ride cymbal with your right hand.

15

Playing a drum set can involve playing up to four surfaces at the same time. So far in this book, you have been playing two surfaces at a time. In the rhythm below, you need to play three together: snare drum, bass drum and ride cymbal. If you find it difficult, try the ride cymbal and snare parts first, then the bass part on its own, before putting it all together.

Repeats in music

A repeat sign tells you to play some of the music again. When you reach a repeat sign, play the music again from the beginning, or from the previous repeat sign if there is one. Ignore the sign the second time you reach it.

Repeat from the beginning of the music.   Repeat the music between these signs.

Born in England in 1947, John **'Mitch' Mitchell** played drums for famous guitarist Jimi Hendrix. Hendrix and his group, the Jimi Hendrix Experience, were well-known for their dramatic, yet controversial, live shows.

Rhythm: Pit stop

When you are playing more than one surface at the same time, make sure you play them exactly together.

Remember to keep counting as you play.

You could try striking your snare drum in different places to create different sounds.

Shorter notes

An eighth note, or quaver, lasts for half a quarter beat. Two or more eighth notes next to each other are often linked together by a line. To count an eighth rhythm, it helps to say "one-and-two-and-three-and-four-and" instead of "one, two, three, four".

 One eighth note lasts for half a quarter beat.

 Two eighth notes last for one quarter beat.

An eighth rest lasts for one eighth beat.

Rhythm: Double up

This piece has a new time signature. In two-four time there are two quarter beats in each measure.

Follow the stickings carefully for the first line. For the last three lines of the piece, play the snare with your left hand and the ride cymbal with your right hand.

Safety

Whenever you play your drum set, it is important to take a few precautions.

Checklist for safety

- Drum sets are loud instruments, so make sure you protect your hearing. Most drum stores stock special ear plugs for drummers, but you can also buy cheap foam ear plugs from most pharmacies.

- Check that you are sitting comfortably with your back straight. Keep your shoulders and arms relaxed.

- It is important to take a break as soon as your fingers, wrists or arms become tired. Playing for a short time every day is better than playing for a long time once a week.

- Make sure all your stands and holders are steady and secure so that nothing can fall over. Keep them in a safe place when you are not using them, where no one is likely to trip over them.

When you strike a drum, as well as the natural thud of the drum, you may also hear a high-pitched ringing sound. This sound usually continues for a short time after the head has been struck. Most drummers use some sort of device to deaden, or dampen, a drum's natural ring. This is known as muffling. Muffling makes a drum sound warmer and more mellow. You can learn more about muffling on page 33, but here you can learn how to muffle your bass drum.

Muffling your bass drum

A bass drum played without any muffling makes a booming, ringing sound. Almost all drummers muffle their bass drum so that it makes a quieter, more solid, thudding sound. Here you can learn about some ways to do this. For some of the methods, you need to remove the resonator head. You can find out how to do this on page 33.

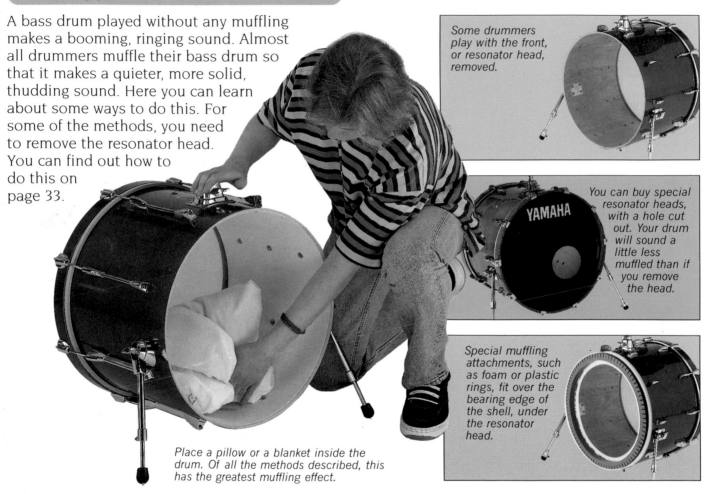

Some drummers play with the front, or resonator head, removed.

You can buy special resonator heads, with a hole cut out. Your drum will sound a little less muffled than if you remove the head.

Special muffling attachments, such as foam or plastic rings, fit over the bearing edge of the shell, under the resonator head.

Place a pillow or a blanket inside the drum. Of all the methods described, this has the greatest muffling effect.

Checklist for muffling your bass drum

- As a general rule, try to use as little muffling as possible. If you muffle the sound too much, your drum will sound too quiet and dull.

- You could try combining different muffling techniques. For example, pillows are often used together with a resonator head that has a hole cut out.

- The amount of muffling you use depends on where you are playing. If you are playing in a small room, you will need to muffle your drum more than if you are playing in a larger room, or auditorium.

- Experiment by muffling your drum in different ways until you are happy with the sound it makes. You could get someone else to listen, as it is often difficult to judge the sound from behind your set.

PLAYING THE HI-HAT

The hi-hat can be used instead of the ride cymbal to play a constant rhythm. Most rock drummers prefer the sound of the hi-hat. It is either played with sticks, or by operating the pedal. When you play it with sticks, you can play with the cymbals closed together or apart.

For the rhythm below, play the hi-hat with your right hand.

To play with the cymbals closed together, you need to keep the pedal pressed down while you are playing. This is called playing in the closed position. You can learn to play with the cymbals apart, called the open position, later in the book. For the rhythm below, strike the closed hi-hat near the middle of the bow, as shown above.

Dave Grohl, born in the USA in 1969, played drums with American band Nirvana, one of the most successful groups of the 90s. In 1995 Grohl recorded an album called *Foo Fighters* almost entirely on his own, not only singing the songs, but playing most of the instruments as well. It was only when the time came to tour that he recruited other musicians and formed the band called Foo Fighters.

Rhythm: Fall-over Francis

For this piece, play the snare with your left hand, while crossing your right hand over your left to play the hi-hat. Press the bass pedal with your right foot and the hi-hat pedal with your left foot. Try practicing one or two measures at a time before playing the whole piece.

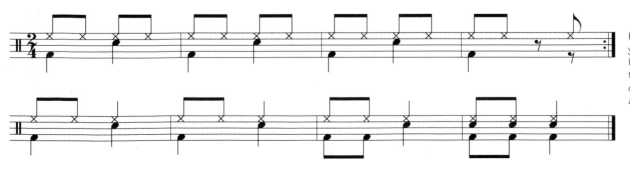

For most pieces, you can play the hi-hat instead of the ride cymbal, or the other way around.

19

PLAYING PATTERNS

You don't have to play lots of flashy solos to be a good drummer. If you listen to the drums in a song, you may notice that the drummer usually plays a short pattern, or figure, which is repeated over and over again. This is known as playing, or keeping, time. Different styles of music, for example rock and blues, each use different patterns.

Born in the USA in 1959, **Sheila E** was discovered by the Artist (formerly known as Prince) in 1984. She has toured and recorded with the Artist as both drummer and vocalist.

Phrases

Music is often divided into short sections called phrases. A phrase is usually a few measures long and can sound like a short piece in itself. Each of the patterns below is one phrase long.

Keeping time

For the patterns below, you need to use the bass drum, snare drum and hi-hat or ride cymbal. Each pattern is made up of a repeated figure that lasts one measure. For all the patterns, play the hi-hat or ride cymbal with your right hand and the snare with your left hand.

Pattern 1

Practice each pattern slowly a few times. Then try playing each one a little faster.

Pattern 2

For this pattern, you could play the ride cymbal instead of the hi-hat.

Pattern 3

Watch out for the eighth notes in the bass drum part.

Pattern 4

For this time signature, count three quarter beats in each measure.

Keeping noise down

Drum sets are loud instruments, so try to consider other people when you are playing. In the checklist below, there are some useful suggestions for ways to keep the noise down. By following them carefully, you can avoid disturbing other people.

Checklist for noise

- Try to practice when you are least likely to disturb anyone else.

- Try not to play too loudly.

- You can practice some things, such as stickings and rhythm, without actually striking anything. Just make the hand movements over your drums and cymbals.

- Muffling your drums makes them sound quieter (see pages 18 and 33).

- You could soundproof your practice area by using heavy curtains, and sealing any gaps around doors and windows.

- You can buy special rubber practice pads to muffle the sound of your drums. These fit on top of the heads of your drums.

- If noise is causing real problems and if your budget allows, you could buy a complete practice set. This is a set of special pads and stands that can be played like a real set, but makes far less noise.

African drums

Most African drums are made from wood or clay, and are either played with sticks or the hands. Since the late 80s, African drums have become very popular in the West. In 1985, American-born singer **Paul Simon** traveled to South Africa where he recorded with well-known African drummers and other musicians, including the group **Ladysmith Black Mambazo**. As a result of these sessions, he recorded the album *Graceland* in 1986. This album helped introduce the rest of the world to African music. The picture above shows Paul Simon singing with Ladysmith Black Mambazo.

At certain points in a piece, most drummers leave the repeated rhythm pattern (see 'Playing patterns' on page 20) and play something new. This usually happens at the ends of phrases. A change in pattern at the end of a phrase is called a 'fill-in' or 'fill'. You can learn about playing fills on this page.

More about repeats

The sign on the right is another repeat sign. When you see it written on the staff, it means that you repeat the music of the previous measure exactly.

Repeat sign

Playing fills

You can use any part of the drum set for fills, but fills played on the toms are most common. You don't have to play a fill at the end of every phrase. A fill, for example, is often played between the verse and chorus of a song. It's a good idea to listen to where other drummers play fills and the type of fills they play. You could start by listening to the drums on your favorite recordings.

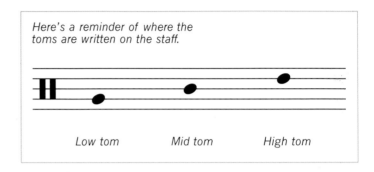

Here's a reminder of where the toms are written on the staff.

Low tom   *Mid tom*   *High tom*

If you only have two toms in your set, you could strike one of the toms twice. But make sure that you finish on the floor tom, or lowest-sounding tom.

Fills can either last for part of the measure, or the whole measure.

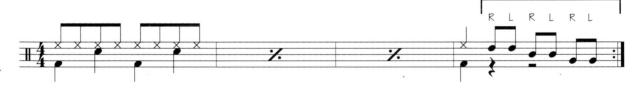

It's a good idea to practice each fill separately before playing them with the patterns.

Try making up your own fills to go with these patterns.

Dotted notes

A dot after a note makes it one and a half times as long. So a dotted half note lasts for three quarter beats, and a dotted quarter note lasts for one and a half quarter beats.

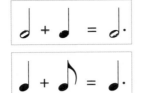

Tied notes

A curved line between two notes on the same line or space is called a tie. Play the first note and hold it for the length of both notes added together.

Don't play this note.

Rhythm: Runaround

This rhythm has a fill at the end of each phrase. When you have practiced it a few times, you could try playing your own fills, instead of the ones written.

For the first line of this piece, play the floor tom with your right hand and the snare with your left hand.

It might help to work out the rhythm before you start to play.

It's a good idea to practice the pattern in the first two measures of the second line a few times.

Playing loudly and quietly

In music, there are Italian words to tell you how loudly or quietly to play. These words are usually shortened to one or two letters. To play loudly, lift your drumstick high above the drum or cymbal, and strike it hard. To play quietly, bring your stick a shorter distance above the surface. Tap it gently, using your fingers to control the stick.

f	Short for forte, *which means "loudly".*
p	Short for piano, *which means "quietly".*
ff	Short for fortissimo, *which means "very loudly" (louder than* forte*).*
pp	Short for pianissimo, *which means "very quietly" (quieter than* piano*).*
mf	Short for mezzo forte, *which means "fairly loud" (quieter than* forte*, but louder than* piano*).*
mp	Short for mezzo piano, *which means "fairly quiet" (louder than* piano*, but quieter than* forte*).*

You can create a variety of sounds by striking different parts of a cymbal. Striking the bell produces a high-pitched 'ping' sound, while striking the edge makes a deeper, crashing sound. In general, the nearer to the bell you play, the tighter the sound, and the nearer to the edge you play, the more the cymbal vibrates and the less definite the sound. Striking your crash cymbal in a different way to your ride cymbal will produce a different sound (see right).

Accents

In drumming, some notes are played louder than others. This is shown on the staff by a special sign called an accent, which is written above or below a note. When you see a note with an accent, strike a little harder.

The crash cymbal

The crash cymbal is often used to provide a crashing sound. It is often used in a fill to make the music sound more exciting and dramatic. Crashes are also used to punctuate a song or a piece of music. For example, a crash is sometimes used to mark the end of a section or the end of a song.

Here's a reminder of where the crash cymbal is written on the staff.

Striking the crash cymbal

To play your crash cymbal, strike it across the edge with the shoulder of your stick. Never strike a cymbal directly on the edge with your stick held straight up, as this can cause the cymbal to crack. Instead, keep your drumstick at roughly a 45° angle, as shown in the picture.

For the rhythm below, use this stroke whenever you play the crash cymbal. You can use either your right or your left hands. If you don't have a crash cymbal, you could strike your ride cymbal as for the crash cymbal.

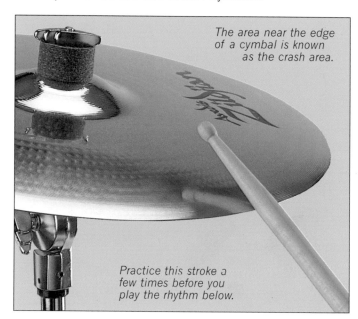

The area near the edge of a cymbal is known as the crash area.

Practice this stroke a few times before you play the rhythm below.

Rhythm: Moving on

For this piece, you might find it easier to play the crash with your right hand.

To play a short crash, simply grab the cymbal in your hand, after you have struck it, to stop the sound.

Sixteenth notes

A sixteenth note is half as long as an eighth note. So two sixteenth notes last for one eighth beat. Groups of sixteenth notes are joined by two lines.

One sixteenth note, or semiquaver

Four sixteenth notes joined together

A sixteenth rest

Rhythm: Roughwork

Sometimes there are notes at the beginning of a piece that don't make up a full bar. These are called upbeats, or pick-ups. The beats in the first and last measures add up to a full measure.

Practice each pattern and fill a few times separately before you play the whole piece.

The bodhrán

The bodhrán is a single-headed drum from Ireland. It is made by stretching an animal-skin head over a wooden frame. This type of drum is often known as a frame drum. There are lots of different types of frame drums and they can be found in most parts of the world.

The bodhrán is usually played with a double-ended stick, but it can also be played with the hands. It is used to accompany Irish dance music, such as reels and jigs, as well as slower tunes. In recent years, lots of Irish bands, such as **The Corrs**, have started to use Irish instruments, including the bodhrán, in their music. The Corrs play a combination of rock and Irish traditional music.

For some songs, you can start with a different rhythm to the main drumming pattern. There are some suggestions for introductions to songs, known as intros, below. When you have played these intros a few times, you could try making up some of your own.

Remember to count the beats as you play.

Intro 1

For this pattern (measures 3-6), you need to play the hi-hat with both hands. Follow the stickings carefully.

Intro 2

Try to play the first beat of each measure a little stronger.

Intro 3

Watch out for the bass drum eighth notes in measure 4.

Intro 4

Richard Starkey, better known as **Ringo Starr,** was born in England in 1940. Starkey played drums with a band called Rory Storm and the Hurricanes, before joining the Beatles in 1962. It was during his years with Rory Storm and the Hurricanes that he acquired the name Ringo Starr: Ringo, because of the rings he wore, and Starr so that his drum solos could be billed as 'Starr time'.

Keith Moon was born in England in 1947 and died in 1978. He joined The Who in 1964, a Mod band well-known for their outrageous stage shows. Moon and the other band members, including guitarist Pete Townsend, frequently trashed their instruments on stage.

ENDINGS

Some songs fade out gradually and never really end, while others have a definite ending. If you are recording a song, it is easy to fade the music out when it reaches the end, but this does not always work so well if you are performing live. Below there are some examples of definite endings to go with the intros and patterns on page 26.

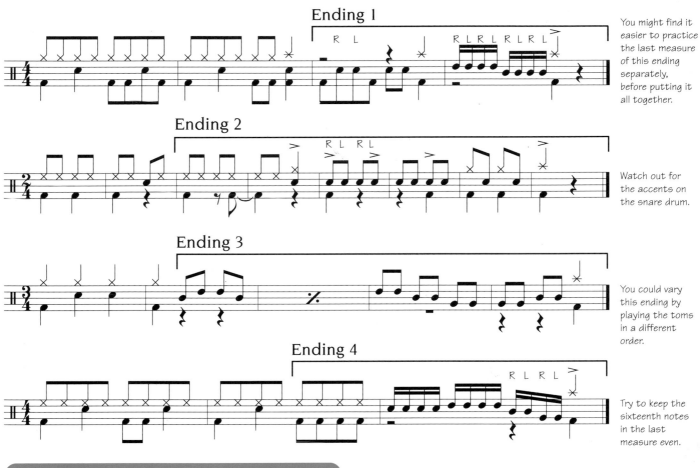

Ending 1

You might find it easier to practice the last measure of this ending separately, before putting it all together.

Ending 2

Watch out for the accents on the snare drum.

Ending 3

You could vary this ending by playing the toms in a different order.

Ending 4

Try to keep the sixteenth notes in the last measure even.

Practicing

There is a lot to take in and remember when you start playing drums. If you practice carefully, however, the things you learn in this book will become much easier. In the checklist below, there are some general rules you can follow to help you get the most from your practice.

Checklist for practicing

- Choose a time when you are not in a hurry and not likely to be disturbed. Make sure you are comfortable and relaxed.

- Play a piece you already know at the beginning of your practice. This will help you to warm up your arms and legs, and to feel confident about your playing.

- Clap the rhythm of each new piece before you play it.

- Practice any hard parts separately, until you can play them well.

- Remember, practicing a little each day is better than playing for a long time once a week.

PLAYING A RIM SHOT

To make pieces sound more interesting, you can strike your drums in different ways. Here you can learn a new drum stroke called a rim shot.

Rim shot

For this stroke, you need to hit the head and the rim of your drum at the same time. Rim shots are usually played on the snare drum, but you can also play them on the toms. A rim shot is a loud and powerful stroke, and is often used as a special effect in fills or solos.

You might find it easier to play a rim shot if you angle your drum away from you slightly.

Leave the snares on for this stroke.

When you feel confident, experiment by striking the drumhead in different places.

Even though a rim shot is played on a drum, it is indicated by a cross in the piece below.

Rhythm: On the edge

In 6/8 time, there are six eighth beats in each measure, arranged in two groups of three. You can either count in eighth notes or dotted quarter notes. There are two dotted quarter notes in each measure.

For a rim shot, make sure you strike both the drumhead and the rim at exactly the same time.

28

PLAYING THE OPEN HI-HAT

So far in this book you have been playing the hi-hat in the closed position. To open the cymbals, you need to raise the foot pedal. Playing with the cymbals apart makes a 'sizzle' sound. They only need to be slightly separated in order to create this effect. Experiment by opening the hi-hat by different amounts. It's a good idea to keep your foot flat on the pedal (see pedal method no.1 on page 15). This makes it easier to control how far apart the cymbals are.

Rhythm: Time out

The open hi-hat is indicated by a 'o' above a note. The closed hi-hat is indicated by a '+' above a note.

For this piece, you need to play the hi-hat in both the open and closed positions.

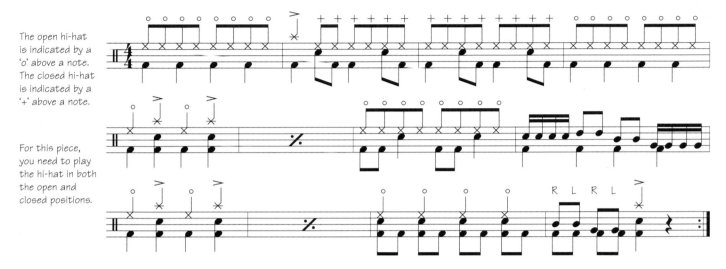

Taking care of your drum set

If you look after your set, you are less likely to have problems with it. See below for some tips.

Checklist for taking care of your drum set

- When you finish playing, cover your drum set with a sheet. If you move your set around, it's a good idea to buy a set of cases for your drums and cymbals.

- Try to keep your drum set away from too much heat. Make sure you don't set it up next to a radiator, or in direct sunlight.

- Check that your drumsticks are not cracked, as splinters or rough edges can damage drumheads and cymbals. Check the bass drum beater regularly for signs of wear.

- Lubricate any movable parts of the bass drum pedal with some household oil.

- Clean your cymbals after use with a soft, dry cloth. Only use a cleaning fluid if it has been recommended by the manufacturer or the store where you bought your drum set.

- Keep some spare felt washers and plastic sleeves handy for your cymbal stands.

- Coat any adjustable parts of your hardware with a thin film of oil. This prevents them from becoming stiff and difficult to adjust.

- If you have a problem with any part of your drum set, get help from the manufacturer or the store where you bought it. Don't try to fix the problem yourself.

DIFFERENT TYPES OF DRUMS AND CYMBALS

There are lots of different types of drums and cymbals. The types you choose depends on the kind of music you want to play, and the sounds you want to create. For a wider range of models, you could look in manufacturers' catalogs. You can use the items shown below just for special effects, or instead of other items in your set (see page 43).

Sizzle cymbals are often used by jazz drummers. This type of cymbal has small pieces of metal, called rivets, set loosely in holes drilled in the bow. When a sizzle cymbal is struck, the vibrations cause the pieces of metal to bounce. This makes a long, sizzling sound. Like other cymbals, the sizzle cymbal can be played on the bell, bow or edge.

Rivets

You could make your own sizzle cymbal by draping the chain of a sink plug over an ordinary cymbal.

The shell of a snare drum is usually made of either wood or metal, and each type makes a different sound.

Piccolo snares are *thinner than ordinary snares so they make a higher sound. Some drummers, especially funk drummers, use piccolo snares instead of, or as well as, regular snares.*

Splash cymbals *are very small, thin cymbals. They are ideal for fast, low-volume crashes.*

Chinese or swish cymbals *have an upturned edge, and are usually used for dramatic, explosive crashes. They can also be played upside down.*

Another way of playing the hi-hat is by pressing and releasing the foot pedal. In the rhythm below, you need to use the hi-hat pedal on beats two and four of each measure. This involves quickly releasing and pressing the pedal on these beats. To operate the pedal, you could try using the 'rocking' method described below.

Here's a reminder of where the note is written when you play the hi-hat with your foot.

Hi-hat rocking method

1. Begin with your foot flat on the pedal, with the cymbals closed together. To play, lift your toe off the pedal to release it, slightly before the beat. Keep your heel at the bottom of the pedal.

2. Press your toe down exactly on the beat, to close the cymbals. At the same time, lift your heel off the pedal. On the next beat, bring your heel back down, but keep the pedal pressed.

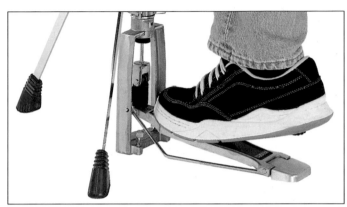

First- and second-time measures

Sometimes a repeated section has two endings. In the rhythm below, there is a pair of measures numbered one and two, called first- and second-time measures. The first time through, play the measure marked "1". The second time through, skip this and play the measure marked "2".

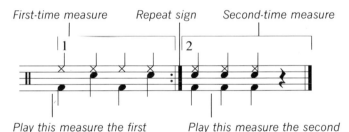

First-time measure   *Repeat sign*   *Second-time measure*

Play this measure the first time through the music.   *Play this measure the second time through the music.*

Rhythm: Ground level

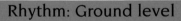

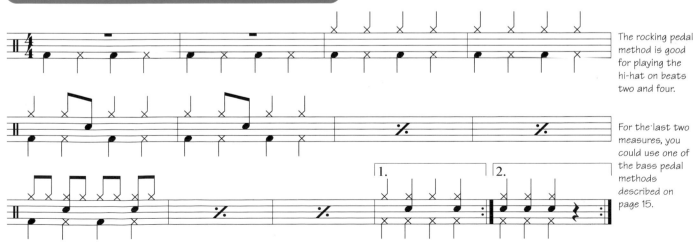

The rocking pedal method is good for playing the hi-hat on beats two and four.

For the last two measures, you could use one of the bass pedal methods described on page 15.

DRUMHEADS

Drumheads don't last forever. They become worn over time and sometimes they just split. Here you can find out about different drumheads and how to replace them.

About drumheads

The type of drumhead you use affects the sound your drum makes. Some heads are thicker or thinner than others. Different manufacturers call drumheads different names, but most heads are made from either one or two layers of plastic. These are called single- or double-ply heads. Layers come in various thicknesses but double-ply heads are usually thicker than single-ply heads. Some heads are coated to make them thicker and stronger.

Clear, single-ply drumhead
This is a thin, uncoated drumhead, made from one layer of plastic.

Coated, double-ply drumhead
This is a thicker head. It is made from two layers of plastic and has a coated surface.

Choosing drumheads

When you buy a drumhead, you need to specify whether it is a batter or a resonator head. The size of head you need depends on the width, or diameter, of your drumshell. To measure this, you need to remove the old drumhead (see page 33). The diameter is the distance from the outside of the wood on one side of the drum to the other (see the diagram below). If, for example, your drumshell diameter is 36cm (14in), you need a drumhead to fit a drum of this size. On the right, there is some advice on choosing drumheads.

To measure the diameter of your drumshell, use the tension brackets as a guide. Measure from one bracket to the one directly opposite.

Checklist for choosing drumheads

- In general, thinner heads make a sharper, brighter sound, while thicker heads make a warmer, more mellow sound.

- Some heads are better for certain styles of playing than others. Thin heads are fragile so they are more suited to quiet, gentle playing. Thicker heads are better for louder, heavy playing. If your drumheads split fairly often, try using thicker ones.

- You don't have to use the same type of head for all of the drums in your set.

- Resonator heads are usually thinner than batter heads, but some can be used for both functions. Be careful though, as some resonator heads, for example, snare heads, are too thin to strike.

- There is a huge variety of drumheads available. If you're not sure which type to buy, ask a music store employee for advice.

Replacing a drumhead

To replace a drumhead you need a drum key, like the one shown below. You can buy keys from drum stores, and most types will fit all of your drums. Once you have replaced a head, you need to stretch it, then tune it. Find out how to do this on pages 34-35.

1. Loosen all the tension screws with your key, but do not pull them out of the counterhoop, or rim.

Try to remember the position of the hoop on the drum before you remove it. The hoop takes the shape of the shell over time, and it will sit best in the same position.   *Drum key*

2. Gently lift the counterhoop away from the drumshell, with the screws still in the holes. Then remove the old drumhead from the shell.

3. Clean inside the shell with a damp cloth. Remove each tension screw, clean it and lubricate it with petroleum jelly. Replace it in the rim before removing the next one.

4. Place the new head on the bearing edge, making sure it fits firmly against it. Line up the logo on the head with the logo on the shell. Place the rim on top of the drumhead.

5. With your drum key, tighten the screws just until you start to feel resistance, or until you can't tighten them any more with your fingers.

Your drum is now ready to be tuned.

More about muffling

As well as your bass drum, you can also muffle the other drums in your set. A simple way of muffling a drum is to stick some strong tape, such as cloth tape, to the side of the drumhead (see below). Alternatively, you could use some of the muffling attachments available, such as plastic or foam rings (see page 18). Some heads are reinforced with plastic or other material, which has a muffling effect on the sound. Below you can see some reinforced drumheads.

Stick some cloth tape to the side of the head. If you want an even more muffled sound, place a piece of tissue under the tape.

Hydraulic drumhead
This head is made from two layers of plastic with a thin coating of oil between the two layers.

Dotted drumhead
The center of this head is reinforced with a round piece of plastic to make it thicker and stronger.

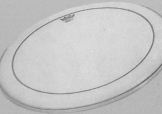

Pinstripe drumhead
This head has a second layer glued on top, the edge of which is marked by a thin black line.

You can change the pitch of a drum by changing the tightness of the drumhead. This is done by adjusting the tension screws on the drum. The tighter the head, the higher the pitch, and the looser the head, the lower the pitch. There are no correct pitches for drums, but some drums sound better at certain pitches than others. By experimenting, you can discover at what pitches your drums sound best. Drums do not need tuning as often as many instruments. However, you do need to tune a drum after you have changed a drumhead.

Stretching a drumhead

The first step in tuning a drum is to stretch the drumhead so that it fits the exact shape of the bearing edge. Start by placing your drum on a carpeted surface, or on a pillow or blanket, with the head you are going to tune facing up.

1. If you have just replaced the head (page 33), make sure that each tension screw is just finger tight. If not, use your key to loosen or tighten each screw to finger tightness.

2. With your drum key, turn each screw one half turn (180°) clockwise, in a criss-cross pattern, following the order shown on the right. This drum has 8 tension screws. Follow the same pattern if your drum has a different number of screws, moving from one tension screw to the one directly opposite.

180°

You could stick a piece of tape on the screw that you started with, so you don't forget where you began.

3. Repeat the criss-cross pattern until any slack or ripples have disappeared. As the head gets tighter, you might want to reduce each turn to one quarter turn (90°).

4. With the palm of your hand, press down firmly in the middle of the head. The bigger the drum, the more pressure you have to apply. You may hear a cracking sound, but don't worry: the head isn't likely to break. Be careful with snare heads though, as they are usually more fragile than other heads.

It's a good idea to press the head down a few times.

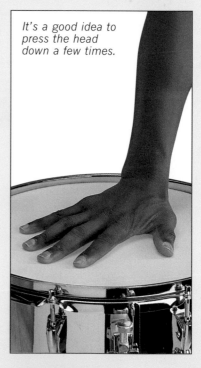

5. When you remove your hand, the head may have slack in it again. Repeat steps 2 and 3 until the slack disappears. Your drum is now ready to tune.

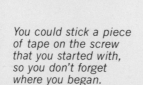

Tuning

To tune your drum, you will need a drumstick as well as your drum key. Whenever you turn the tension screws, follow the criss-cross pattern shown on the previous page. Once you have tuned a drum, it may stretch a bit more, so you might want to fine tune it about once a day for a few days until the head settles.

Listen very carefully to the pitch produced at each point on the drumhead. You might find it helpful to sing each one.

1. With your stick, tap a point on the head one or two inches in from each tension screw. Each point may produce a different pitch.

2. Tighten or loosen the tension screws with your key, until you hear the same pitch at each point.

Remember to follow the criss-cross pattern.

3. Now tune your drum to the pitch you want, by turning each tension screw one quarter turn at a time. Check that each point produces the same pitch. For double-headed drums, you need to stretch and tune the opposite head also. You can either tune it to the same pitch as the opposite head, or you can tune it slightly higher.

Checklist for tuning drums

- In a drum set, the snare drum usually has the highest pitch, and the bass drum the lowest. The toms are tuned between these pitches, with the floor tom being the lowest (but higher than the bass drum), the medium rack tom a little higher, and the small rack tom the highest (lower than the snare drum).

- Tuning your drums carefully can make a huge difference to the sounds they produce. Experiment with different tunings until you are happy with the sounds your drums make.

- If a drum keeps going out of tune, it could be damaged. If this happens, it is best to get help from the store where you bought it, or the manufacturer. Don't try to fix the problem yourself.

East Indian drums

The group **Cornershop** include both Western and Indian instruments in their band, and Indian drums and rhythms play a major part in their music. The group uses different types of Indian drums, including a pair of small drums called tablā, which are played with the hands.

The picture shows a large double-headed barrel drum. Striking this drum with different parts of the hands and fingers will produce different sounds. Cornershop's music is a mixture of popular Western styles, such as hip-hop, and traditional Indian music.

PLAYING IN DIFFERENT STYLES

On the next few pages there are some rhythms in different styles such as jazz, blues, funk and reggae. Learning to play in different styles will broaden your knowledge of music and improve your technical skills. You can also learn new drumming patterns that might be useful if you want to start making up your own music.

Triplets

Triplets are indicated by a '3' above or below a group of three notes. A triplet sign tells you to play three notes in the time of two. So you play three triplet eighth notes in the time of two eighth notes, or one quarter note. Blues rhythms often use triplets (see below).

American-born, **Al Jackson Jr.** (1934-1975) began playing drums on stage, with his father's band, at the age of five. In 1962, he joined the blues and soul band, Booker T and the MGs (short for 'Memphis Group'). While recording, Jackson often muffled his snare drum by placing his wallet on the drumhead.

Blues drumming

Blues was developed in the late 19th century in the south of the USA. The rhythm below is a typical blues pattern using eighth triplets.

Rhythm: Rollin'

The word "simile" tells you to continue playing triplets wherever you see a group of three eighth notes.

You don't need to play this rhythm very fast.

For the last measure, you might find it easier to play the bass pedal using the toe method (see page 15).

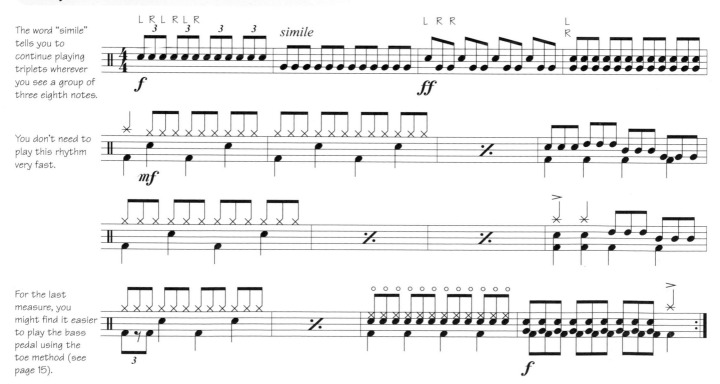

36

JAZZ DRUMMING

The pieces below are based on a fairly typical jazz pattern, using a triplet figure. In each triplet group, the middle note is replaced by a rest, giving the rhythm a 'swing' feel. You can play 'Sewn up' on your snare using brushes. Brushes are made of strands of wire or plastic bound together, and they are used to create a soft 'swish' sound. It is important that your snare has a coated drumhead, not a smooth one.

Using brushes

The diagrams in the pictures below show the movements for your right and left hands. You can hold your brushes using either the matched or traditional grips.

Keep your left brush on the head all the time, moving clockwise in a circle. Each circle should last for one quarter note. Keep a regular quarter beat, starting at the position shown.

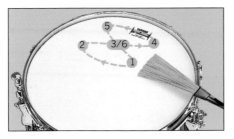

The right brush plays the triplet figure (see 'Sewn up' below). Strike the head in different places instead of keeping the brush on it. Follow the pattern shown in the diagram on the left.

Drummer **Elvin Jones** was born in the USA in 1927. He rose to fame, however, through his partnership with saxophone player John Coltrane, with whom he made a series of albums in the 60s. During this time he contributed to some of the most influential, yet controversial, jazz music. Jones often uses lots of complicated rhythms that echo African drumming.

Rhythm: Sewn up

The left-hand swish is indicated by an arrow.

Play the last measure with brushes too.

Rhythm: Nice 'n' easy

For this piece, keep the tip of your stick fairly close to the ride cymbal.

LATIN DRUMMING

Latin music usually means the music of South and Central America, as well as that of the Caribbean islands. In lots of Latin rhythms, the emphasis is not always on the main beats of the measure, making the music very rhythmic and energetic. This off-beat rhythm is known as syncopation.

Here are two Latin rhythms for you to play. Try playing the snare drum with the snares off. This is a technique often used in Latin music.

On the right you can learn about the cross-stick rim shot, a drum stroke which is used in Latin drumming. In the rhythms below, this stroke is written in the same way as an ordinary rim shot (see page 28), but with C.S. written over the note.

Cross-stick rim shot

The cross-stick rim shot is a variation of the rim shot, and is usually played on the snare drum. For this shot, the tip of the stick rests on the head, while the shaft is used to strike the rim. Keep your fingers on the head as shown below.

Rhythm: Bossa nova

It's a good idea to practice the ride and bass parts together before adding the snare.

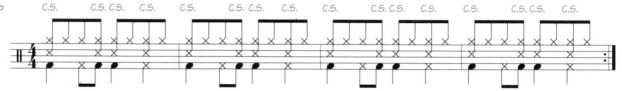

Rhythm: Samba

There are two different patterns in this piece. Try practicing each one separately.

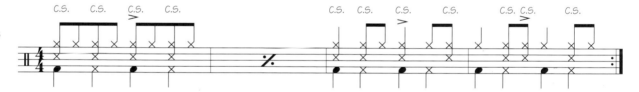

Born Ernesto Antonio Puente Jnr., **Tito Puente** was born in the USA in 1923. From the 30s, Puente featured with many Latin orchestras as drummer and percussionist, often playing Latin drums called timbales. He formed his own band in the late 40s, which reached the height of its popularity during the 50s and 60s. Puente is probably one of the best and most popular Latin drummers and percussionists.

REGGAE

Reggae music originated in Jamaica during the 1960s. It became popular in the USA and Europe through the recordings of artists such as Bob Marley. It usually consists of short repeated patterns played on electric guitars, bass guitars, keyboards and drums. Like Latin music, reggae music often uses the cross-stick rim shot.

Rhythm: Black coffee

Triplet patterns, like the one in this piece, are often a feature of reggae drumming. Syncopated rhythms are also used in reggae music, and the cross-stick rim shot is sometimes used to emphasise the off-beats. As you play this rhythm, remember to count the quarter notes evenly and try not to rush the triplets.

Born Lowell Charles Dunbar in Jamaica in 1952, **Sly Dunbar** (left) is best known for his work with bass player, Robbie Shakespeare (right). Since the 70s, the pair, known as Sly and Robbie, have dominated the world of reggae music with their inventive playing.

You don't need to play this piece very quickly.

Try to keep a steady speed.

ELECTRONIC DRUMS

Drum machines

Drum machines are electronic devices that store and play back the sounds of percussion instruments. Using these sounds, you can create rhythm patterns. Lots of dance music styles, such as techno, use beats generated by drum machines, instead of regular, or acoustic, drum sets.

On most drum machines, you can create your own percussion sounds.

You can choose sounds and play rhythms by tapping on the pads.

Electronic drum sets

Electronic drum sets consist of a set of special rubber- or plastic-coated pads, one for each item of an acoustic set. Just as each surface in an acoustic set produces a different sound, each pad in an electronic set can be programmed to make a different sound. Electronic sets can also be programmed to play rhythm patterns. They are often used for dance music, such as techno and jungle. Some drummers combine electronic and acoustic drums and cymbals as part of their setup. This gives a much wider range of sounds.

Electronic drum set

Each pad is connected to a computer that creates the various sounds.

Born in England in 1964, **Andy Gangadeen** has played drums for various bands including M-People, Massive Attack and the Spice Girls. More recently, he has concentrated on different styles of dance music. Using a combination of acoustic and electronic drums, he plays entire compositions himself, including all of the melody parts.

FUNK

Funk has its roots in African and gospel music, but also contains elements of different styles such as jazz. Funk evolved in the USA in the 1960s, with the music of artists such as James Brown and Sly and the Family Stone. The pieces below are two funk rhythms for you to play.

Rhythm: Cover up

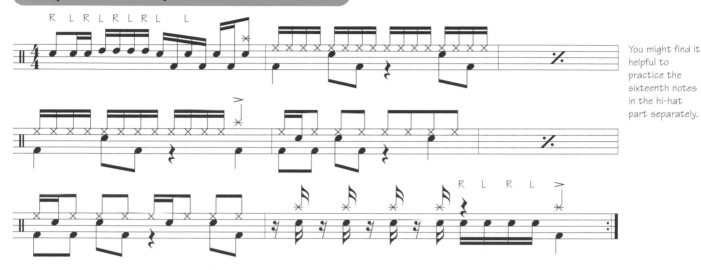

You might find it helpful to practice the sixteenth notes in the hi-hat part separately.

Rhythm: Lifeline

At the end of each measure of this piece, strike the hi-hat while releasing the pedal. On the first beat of the next measure, strike it as you are pressing the pedal. This makes a 'shoop' sound.

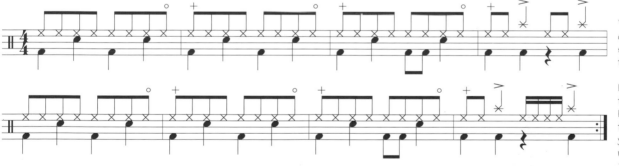

You only need to open the hi-hat slightly to create the shoop sound.

It's a good idea to practice the hi-hat shoop technique before you play the whole piece.

Billy Cobham was born in the USA in 1944. In the late 60s, he joined John McLaughlin's Mahavishnu Orchestra, one of the most influential and highly-regarded jazz-rock bands of the 60s and 70s. In 1973, Cobham formed his own band and continued to lead jazz and funk groups for the next few years. He has often been described as one of the most accomplished funk drummers.

SOLOS

Sometimes the drummer in a band plays a solo. Most drummers see this as a chance to show off their skills as a player. Solos usually involve leaving the steady pattern of the piece to introduce new rhythms, using a variety of different drums and cymbals. Here are some solos for you to play. When you can play them confidently, you could try making up some of your own. Try to make your solo as interesting as possible, but always make sure it fits in with the rest of the music. You don't need to use lots of different drumming techniques or complicated rhythms. Only use the rhythms and techniques you feel confident with.

Rhythm: Out-take

Try playing this a little faster when you are sure of the rhythm.

Rhythm: Limelight

For this solo, try to work out the stickings yourself.

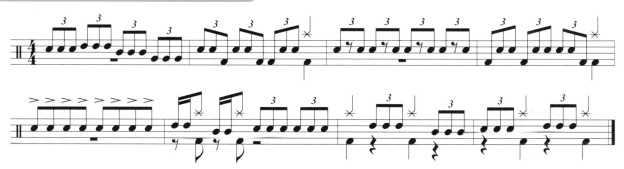

Ginger Baker played drums for the band Cream, one of the most influential rock bands of the 60s. Together with guitarist Eric Clapton, and bass guitarist Jack Bruce, Baker helped pave the way for hard rock bands such as Led Zeppelin and artists such as Jimi Hendrix. The group's live performances included complex, impressive solos by all three members that often lasted over 20 minutes. One of Baker's favourite sets was one he made himself from strong plastic. It was smashed up by Jack Bruce in an argument on stage.

There is no standard number of drums and cymbals in a drum set. It is up to you how big or small you want your set to be. Some drummers play enormous, flashy sets, made up of a huge range of drums and cymbals, while others prefer the bare essentials.

Buying lots of new equipment is expensive, so think carefully about which items you want and why you want them. Remember that you can make different sounds by experimenting with the items you already have. For example, you could strike surfaces in different ways, using different parts of your drumsticks.

Extras

Depending on the sound you want to create, you could add a second bass, snare or hi-hat. There are various pedal systems available that, for example, allow you to play two bass drums at the same time. You can also get a wide variety of sounds by adding more toms or more cymbals of different weights and sizes.

English-born **John Bonham** (1947-1980) played drums with the heavy metal band Led Zeppelin. Bonham often made up rhythms as he went along, especially in his solos. One of his most famous solos was from the song *Moby Dick*.

This drum set includes a variety of cymbals of different weights and sizes.

If you are adding extra toms, place them in order according to their size.

Some funk drummers use a piccolo snare for special effects, as well as a regular snare.

You could add some of the different types of drums and cymbals shown on page 30.

Any special-effects items should be within reach but not as close as items that you use regularly, such as the ride cymbal.

DRUMMING PATTERNS

Being able to play a wide variety of drumming patterns is very useful if you want to play with other musicians, or in a band. Try to learn the patterns on this page from memory if you can. You could try making up an intro, some fills, and an ending to go with some of them.

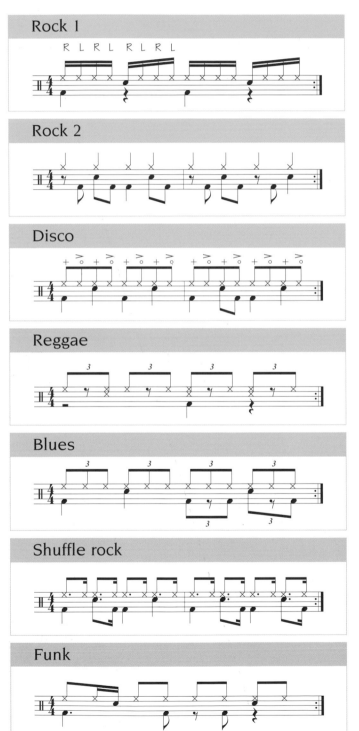

Rock 1

Rock 2

Disco

Reggae

Blues

Shuffle rock

Funk

Latin

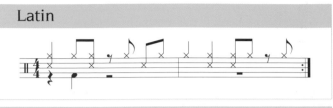

Latin rock

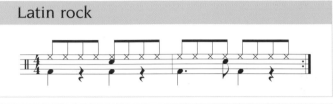

Jazz

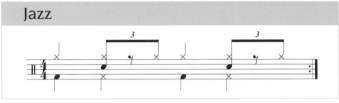

Heavy metal

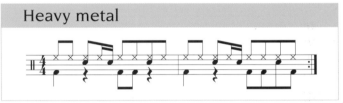

Drummer **Charlie Watts** was born in England in 1941. Primarily a jazz musician, Watts joined the Rolling Stones, somewhat reluctantly, in the early 60s. He is known for his great timekeeping.

MAKING UP YOUR OWN MUSIC

Making up music as you go along is called improvising. As a drummer in a band, you may have to improvise drum beats for the songs that your band wants to play. It takes time to learn to improvise, but the more you practice and experiment, the easier it becomes. On this page there are some guidelines to help you.

Following a song

Start by figuring out the time signature of the song. Next, choose a drum pattern in this time signature, in the style of the song. You could play one of the patterns on the previous page, or you could make up one of your own. See the checklist on the right for some ideas.

Thinking about structure

Think carefully about how to start and end the song. If you need to play an intro by yourself, try to start with something interesting to catch the listeners' attention. The most common type of song is a verse/chorus song. Lots of drummers use the same pattern for each verse. Sometimes the verse and chorus are linked by a short section called a bridge. Try to make the bridge and chorus sound different from the verse by using different rhythms, or a different combination of drums and cymbals. Be selective about where and when you add fills.

Checklist for following a song

- Listen carefully to the other instruments and make sure your part suits the music the other instruments are playing.

- Experiment by using different combinations of drums and cymbals, and different patterns.

- Don't overload the music with special techniques and complicated rhythms. This can make the music sound confused.

- Add variety by playing a rhythm pattern in slightly different ways for different parts of the song. Some parts may sound better without any drums at all.

- Decide where you need to play loudly and where you need to play softly. Make sure you don't drown out the other instruments.

- It's a good idea to record the song on a cassette. Then listen to how your drumming works with the song and the other instruments in the band.

American rock band The Velvet Underground was formed in 1964. Drummer **Maureen 'Mo' Tucker**, born in 1945 in the USA, joined the group in 1965. She often used experimental drumming techniques, such as turning her bass drum horizontal and playing it with drumsticks instead of using the foot pedal. Although not a mainstream group, The Velvet Underground became one of the most influential bands of the 60s, inspiring many 80s groups such as Joy Division and The Jesus and Mary Chain. Many Velvet Underground songs dealt with controversial social issues.

PLAYING IN A BAND

Here is a piece for you to play with other people. If you know some people who play keyboards and rhythm guitar, they could use the chords above the bass guitar part as a guide. The guitar parts are written with tablature (another way of writing guitar music) as well as on a staff.

Chant (lead guitar part)

Make sure the instruments are in tune with each other. If you are playing with a keyboard player, you should all tune your instruments to the keyboard.

If you get lost, you could follow another part and join in later. To help you, the measures are numbered at the beginning of each staff.

Chant (bass guitar part)

If you don't know anyone who has a bass guitar, you could try playing this part on the bottom four strings of an ordinary guitar.

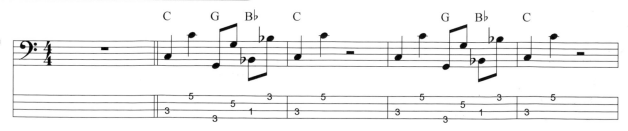

(Bass guitar part continued)

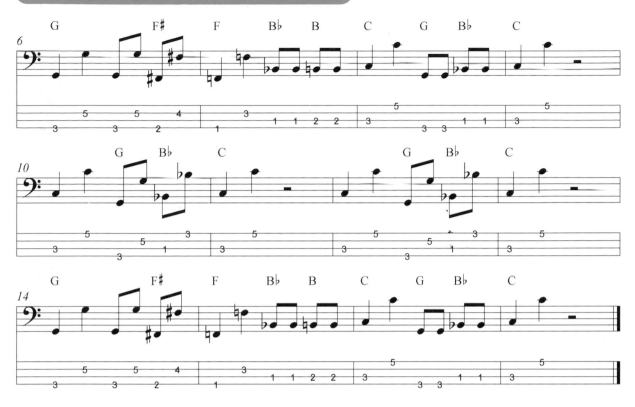

Chant (drums part)

Make sure you decide on a speed with the other players before you begin.

INDEX

Acknowledgements

The publishers would like to thank the following for supplying the instruments and drumming equipment used in the photos: Yamaha-Kemble Music (UK) Ltd.; Avedis Zildjian Company; Remo Inc.; J. D'Addario & Company, Inc./Evans; Chas E. Foote Ltd., London. The publishers are grateful to the following for the use of their photographic material:
Redferns (page 3, Phil Collins; page 4, Chad Smith; page 14, Peter Erskine; page 19, Dave Grohl; page 25, The Corrs; page 26, Keith Moon; page 35, Cornershop; page 41, Billy Cobham; page 42, Ginger Baker). *Retna* (page 21, Paul Simon/Ladysmith Black Mambazo). *London Features International*

Ltd. (page 16, Mitch Mitchell; page 20, Sheila E; page 36, Al Jackson Jr.; page 38, Tito Puente; page 39, Sly and Robbie; page 44, Charlie Watts; page 45, Maureen 'Mo' Tucker). *Pictorial Press* Ltd. (page 26, Ringo Starr; page 43, John Bonham). *Val Wilmer* (page 37, Elvin Jones). *Rhythm/James Cumpsty* (page 40, Andy Gangadeen). *Clavia Digital Musical Instruments* AB (page 40, electronic drum kit). *Yamaha-Kemble Music (UK) Ltd.* (page 40, drum machine; page 43, drum set).
The drummers in the photographs were: Isaac Quaye, Mark Howlett, Mike Wheatley and Steve Wright.
With thanks to Pod Trademarks Partnership.